GODZILLA

Yasuhiko Ohashi
GODZILLA

Translated by
M. Cody Poulton

Godzilla
first published 2002 by
Scirocco Drama
An imprint of J. Gordon Shillingford Publishing Inc.
© 1987 Yasuhiko Ohashi
© 2002 English Translation M. Cody Poulton
Reprinted 2010, 2018

Scirocco Drama Editor: Glenda MacFarlane
Cover design by Terry Gallagher/Doowah Design Inc.
Author photo by Toshi Aoyagi
Translator's photo by Fisheye Photography

Printed and bound in Canada on 100% post-consumer recycled paper.

We acknowledge the financial support of the Manitoba Arts Council, The Canada Council for the Arts and the Government of Canada through the Book Publishing Industry Development Program (BPIDP) for our publishing program.

All rights reserved. No part of this book may be reproduced, for any reason, by any means, without the permission of the publisher. This play is fully protected under the copyright laws of Canada and all other countries of the Copyright Union and is subject to royalty. Changes to the text are expressly forbidden without written consent of the author. Rights to produce, film, record in whole or in part, in any medium or in any language, by any group amateur or professional, are retained by the author.
Production inquiries should be addressed to:
M. Cody Poulton
1009 Terrace Avenue
Victoria, BC, Canada
V8S 3V2

Canadian Cataloguing in Publication Data

Ohashi, Yasuhiko, 1956-
    Godzilla/Yasuhiko Ohashi; translated by M. Cody Poulton
A play.
Translated from the Japanese.
ISBN 1-896239-96-X

    1. Godzilla (Fictitious character)—Drama. 2. Ohashi, Yashuhiko, 1956- Translations into English. I. Poulton, Mark Cody, 1955- II. Title.
PL858.H38G6313 2002   895.6'25   C2002-903973-8

J. Gordon Shillingford Publishing
P.O. Box 86, RPO Corydon Avenue, Winnipeg, MB Canada R3M 3S3

Author's Preface

Over all these years, how many buildings has he toppled?

And how many rockets and missiles has his body had to withstand?

And how many tanks has he crushed underfoot?

This is a story of another kind about the one they call the "king of the monsters."

—Yasuhiko Ohashi

Yasuhiko Ohashi

Yasuhiko Ohashi was born in 1956 and founded his theatre troupe Libresen (Freedom Boat) in 1983. *Godzilla* was written and directed by Ohashi in 1987, and received the Kishida Kunio Drama Award in 1988. Ohashi's major theatre works are *Camellia Flower* (1993), a time travel story which goes back to the moment of the famous suicide by an advertising copywriter in the 1970s, and *Original* (2001), semi-horror stories of bodies invaded by lost souls. Ohashi is also a regular writer for NHK television, Japan's national public broadcasting station. A cultural staple, *Godzilla* has toured repeatedly throughout Japan.

M. Cody Poulton

M. Cody Poulton teaches Japanese literature and theatre at the University of Victoria, Canada. Recent publications include *Spirits of Another Sort: The Plays of Izumi Kyôka* (2001). He is also the translator of three kabuki plays in Vols. I and II of *Kabuki Plays on Stage* (2002) and two contemporary plays for Vols. IV and V of *Half A Century of Japanese Theater* (2002, 2003).

Production Credits

Godzilla's English language premiere was on September 19, 2002 at Toronto's Factory Theatre Studio Café, produced by Crow's Theatre, with the following cast:

YAYOI		Melinda Deines
NARRATOR/EIJI TSUBAURAYA		Paul Sun-Hyung Lee
TWIN SISTERS	Emi	Susan Doyon
	Yumi	Hilary Doyle
MOTHER		Tracey Hoyt
FATHER		Keith Knight
GRANDMOTHER		Jean Yoon
HAYATA		Shawn Mathieson
TV REPORTER/PIGMON		Diana Tso
GODZILLA		John O'Callaghan
MOTHRA		Gene Mack

Directed by Jim Millan
Associate Director: Susan Doyon
Lighting and Sound Design by Spencer Hazel
Set Design by Sherri Hay
Costume Design by Sarah Armstrong
Production Manager: Roger West
Stage Manager: Fiona Kennedy
Producer: Lyndee Hansen

Characters

The Ichinose Family:	Monsters:	Others:
FATHER, Yôgan ICHINOSE	GODZILLA	HAYATA, *a policeman*
MOTHER, Tsumugi	MOTHRA	TV REPORTER
GRANDMOTHER	PIGMON	NARRATOR
YAYOI		Eiji TSUBURAYA, *a film director*

TWIN SISTERS, Emi *and* Yumi

Note from the playwright: All said and done, this play is a work for the stage. Play Godzilla and the other monsters with real actors —no rubber suits, please. If the audience means well and is imaginative, Godzilla will look like Godzilla...

The version of this story is set three years after Godzilla's silver screen comeback in 1984, but feel free to update the topical references in each production.

Translator's Introduction

Yasuhiko Ohashi's play *Godzilla* was first performed in 1987 and won Japan's top drama prize, the Kishida Kunio Award, the following year. Japan was then riding a crest of unprecedented prosperity, with a booming economy and soaring stock values. Though the strong yen put a brake on exports, the quality of Japanese manufactured products continued to ensure a worldwide market for them; by the same token, imports of luxury items never seemed cheaper and foreign travel and investment were affordable to ever greater numbers of Japanese people. Japanese corporations were buying up American icons like the Rockefeller Center and Paramount Studios. The major cities were in the throes of an orgy of property speculation: it was said at one point in the late 1980s that the current market real estate value of the greater Tokyo metropolitan area was equivalent to that of all of the United States. Japan had seemingly become a hedonistic and media-driven society, interested only in speed—quickness of thought and image, the passing rather than the permanent.

What a change from the Japan of 1954, when Tôhô Pictures released the first in a long series of *Godzilla* films. Less than a decade earlier, the country had been devastated, its infrastructure destroyed and its major cities turned into wastelands by nuclear and incendiary bombs. Japan in 1954 had just shaken off the U.S. Occupation and was busy rebuilding, but few had time to enjoy themselves and practically everyone had vivid memories of the wartime destruction. The giant reptile Godzilla, released from its icy slumber by an American hydrogen bomb test, reminded the Japanese not only of their recent past but also of the precariousness of their future in the nuclear age. Since that time some two dozen films have ensured that Godzilla has become star in a bestiary (if not pantheon) of the contemporary Japanese popular imagination. In sequel after sequel, Godzilla has gone up against men and other monsters, both domestic and foreign—the Japanese Self-Defense Forces, the Americans and Russians, Mothra (1961, 1964), King Kong (1962), King Ghidorah (1964), Daimajin (1966), Hedorah (1971), and Mechagodzilla (1974), to name just a few. Like Frankenstein, he exists as an apocalyptic warning of what the untrammeled pursuit of scientific progress may hold in store for humanity. His perennial popularity no doubt betrays something of the insecurity that Japanese have continued to feel, despite their phoenix-like rise from the ashes of defeat in 1945. Recently the Tarô Okamoto Museum in Kawasaki City devoted a solemn exhibition to this monster.

As member of the selection committee that awarded Yasuhiko Ohashi the Kishida Prize, playwright Hisashi Inoue noted that "we all have our own stories about Godzilla."[1] Ohashi (who was born in 1956) was no different from any young Japanese boy of his generation: twice a year, during the summer and at year-end, he looked forward to the release of yet another sequel. A graduate of electrical engineering at the Musashi Institute of Technology, Ohashi's interest in theatre was developed building props and sets in the campus theatre club. In 1983, together with fellow playwright Yumiko Itô and others, he established the theatre company Freedom Boat (Libresen), for which he continues to serve as artistic director and house playwright. Ohashi is famous for his special stage effects and spectacular set design, often accomplished with minimum financial outlay. He has said that when writing a play, he begins with the theatre space itself and asks himself how it can best be imaginatively filled. His first important work, *The Red Bird Escaped* (Akai tori nigeta, 1986), was based on the August 1985 crash of a Japan Airlines jumbo jet that claimed 520 lives, at that time the worst disaster in civil aviation history. Ohashi's plays are typical of much post-1960s Japanese theatre: highly physical collages that demonstrate a fiuid sense of time and space; an eclectic mix of both cultural references (Western and Japanese, traditional, modern and popular) and dramatic genres (romance, farce, comedy, tragedy) in playful and often absurdist ways. Like many of his contemporaries, he experiments in complex, multi-level dramatic structures that juxtapose reality and dream. Yet, in contrast to the plays of Hideki Noda, for example, his theatre is distinguished by a strong narrative backbone and an elegiac lyricism.

Godzilla is first and foremost a love story, a romantic comedy about a young Japanese woman who falls in love with a giant lug.

Ohashi makes it clear from the outset that he is not interested, however, in depicting Godzilla literally as the monster of the Tôhô films: his stage notes specify that no rubber suits or special effects other than lighting and sound are to be employed. Godzilla in this play should appear to the audience as a man, though to the woman's family he remains a loathsome lizard. Every parent who has a daughter worries about what kind of man their girl will bring home, and Ohashi exaggerates and satirizes those anxieties by turning the suitor into (next to the Americans) Japan's biggest boogeyman of all. The playwright has also suggested that Godzilla is an embodiment of the kind of masculine strength and stoicism that men of his generation have for the most part lost. Beneath the violence of his character, however, there lies a gentleness and sensitivity that appeals to the girl Yayoi, who herself is an unreal ideal of all that is pure and innocent in women. This "Beauty and the Beast" motif resonates with the Japanese, who have deep memories in their folklore and traditional drama of stories about men and women who mate with spirits and gods disguised as cranes, foxes, snakes, and other animals. The popularity of this motif no doubt has to do with its ability to dramatize in symbolic terms long-standing concerns about race or ethnicity, class and gender: the opposite sex often seemed like another species (men are from Mars!), especially when one's lover came from another village or social order, with its own language, customs and traditions.

Contrasted to these pure archetypes of masculinity and femininity represented by Godzilla and Yayoi is the girl's family, who are superficial, vulgar, greedy and hypocritical—in short, a parody of everything that contemporary Japanese society has become. From the outset we learn that there is a huge gap between the Ichinose family cant about tradition, propriety and status and how they actually behave. The father Yôgan is particularly keen to marry his daughters off to well-born high achievers in order to escape from his own humble, debt-ridden predicament. In asking for men who are also strong, he is, however, getting more with Yayoi's fiancé than he had bargained for. The mother is a mousy caricature of the modern housewife and Yayoi's little sisters, the twins Emi and Yumi, are Japanese valley girls whose arch attitude and materialistic dreams have been manufactured by the mass media. Ohashi takes numerous jabs in this play at Japanese commercial television, whose chattering newscasters and amateurish entertainers (called in Japan, oxymoronically, "talents") often make North American TV seem positively enlightened. Only the grandmother, who herself fesses up to a couple of flings with animals when she was young, hints at deeper levels of sympathy and imagination than her shallow relatives.

If *Godzilla* is a satire on the modern Japanese family system and its marriage customs, Yayoi's gargantuan fiancé has his own genealogy that is a gentle poke at the cornier side of Japanese disaster and science fiction movies. The play features a fantasy sequence, the wedding of Yayoi and Godzilla, in which Godzilla's "family"—his brother and sister, the monsters Mothra and Pigmon, and their father, Eiji Tsuburaya (1901-1970), original creator of many of the monsters and special effects for these films—makes an appearance. When Mothra makes his entrance as a caterpillar, the Ichinose twins suddenly become the hit 1960s female twin pop duo, The Peanuts, and sing the production number that gave them considerable camp immortality, from the 1964 film *Godzilla vs. Mothra*. Later, Yayoi's childhood friend and jealous suitor, Hayata, is transformed into Ultraman, the superhero of a popular '60s television series developed by Tsuburaya Productions. Like Superman, Ultraman hails from another planet and passes himself off as a human (also called Hayata in the TV series) until duty calls. His transformation into Ultraman can last for only three minutes, however; any longer and he would die.

Ohashi's play was written on the heels of the 1984 remake of *Godzilla*, a film that marked the fiftieth anniversary of Tôhô Pictures and, incidentally, the end of a near decade-long hiatus from *Godzilla* movie making. Like the James Bond films, however, the *Godzilla* series had over time become a parody of itself and, despite the hype, the remake elevated the genre to new levels of kitsch and camp. Godzilla goes against a high-tech airship called Super X and (as he does in the 1954 original) finally dies in a shower of lava on the volcanic Mount Mihara. Two years, later, in 1986, life imitated art and Mount Mihara (situated on Oshima Island, directly to the south of metropolitan Tokyo) erupted, forcing the evacuation of its inhabitants. Television images of fleeing islanders, coupled with similar scenes from the *Godzilla* movies, were the raw material for Ohashi's imagination.

A Note on Names:

Names of people, real or fictional, are given in the Western style, i.e., personal name first and family name last, though the Japanese custom is to reverse that order. Japanese pronunciation is similar to Italian or Spanish. There are only five vowel sounds (a, i, u, e, o) and no diphthongs, as there are in English. Every syllable is voiced, with little obvious stress on any one syllable. Hence, Ichinose is pronounced "Ichinosé" and Yayoi is counted as three syllables. The name Eiji is pronounced like "agey," or the letters "AG"; Daiei sounds like "die, eh." Consonants are more or less as in English, but "g" is always hard (as in "Garry," not "George"). "Hatchan" is a diminutive form of "Hayata-san" (Mr. Hayata)—the former indicates a fair degree of affection for the character. There are a number of untranslatable puns on characters' names: Yayoi means "April"; the father's name, Yôgan, can also mean "lava"; the mother's name, Tsumugi, refers to a style of weaving, called pongee in English, for which Oshima Island is famous. Godzilla is said to be an amalgam of two words: gorilla and *kujira* (whale). A couple of other monster names mentioned have a similar pedigree: Gamakujira is a cross between a toad (*gama*) and a whale (*kujira*), Namegon is derived from *namakuji* (slug) and Ebirah is a shrimp (*ebi*) monster.

The translation and acknowledgements:

An earlier translation of this play, by John Gillespie, is available in Japan Playwrights Association, ed. *Half A Century of Japanese Theater III: the 1980s Part 1* (Kinokuniya, 2001). That translation was adapted by Toshi Aoyagi and Susan Doyon for a dramatic reading of the play by Crow's Theatre at the Japan Foundation, Toronto, in January 2002. The present work, a completely new translation, was commissioned by Crow's Theatre for the first full Canadian production of the play at the Factory Theatre Studio Café in Toronto, September-October 2002. (The translation used in the stage production may differ slightly from this published version.) The translator wishes to thank the playwright, co-director of the dramatic reading Susan Doyon, and director of the stage production Jim Millan for their invaluable assistance in revising this text. Thanks, too, to AT for getting this lizard to fly, and to my wife Mitsuko, as always, for her patience.

Cody Poulton, Victoria, British Columbia, July 29, 2002

Endnotes

[1] Hisashi Inoue, "Monogatari no kankiryoku" (The power to awaken stories), *Shingeki*, March 1988.

Scene One
The Pier/ Yayoi's Love

> *An unsettled atmosphere of cacophonous sounds: boat whistles, waves, traffic congestion, sirens. A pale yellow light dimly illuminates the scene, as in a faded photo of sepia tones.*
>
> *In the far distance, the echo of a loud explosion. A young woman appears, bathed in a variety of colours, like fireworks on a summer night.*
>
> *The port of Oshima Motomachi. The rescue ship Katori is taking on the last of the island's refugees. Fearing what might come, the boat is wasting no time in starting up the engine and leaving the port.*

YAYOI: It was like I was all wrapped up in the faint scent of camellias. He said nothing, just looked deep into my eyes, as gentle as a spring day that goes on forever. His eyes were so big I could see my whole body reflected in them. What is he trying to tell me? Somehow I just knew. It's been half a year now since we first met and though I'll go on singing the praises of our little old love to the skies, I still can't quite say we're a perfect match.

I'm just an ordinary girl. All I want is to sit in some trendy café over a cup of coffee, nattering on about myself and trying to impress him; or squeeze his hand, pretending to be afraid at some boring horror flick; or cuddle up on a sandy beach at night and, swept away by the sweet waves and the salty breeze, give myself up to his mad kisses. I know it's banal, but still, I want dates like that. But I can't. Why, you ask? Because, well, after all, he's...Godzilla.

We'd meet in the dead of night on Mt. Mihara, when all the tourists had gone. It took me five minutes to catch up to his every step, but he never complained. He always had a smile for me and quietly waited, watching me scurry along. Even when we sat down together, there were still some thirty meters between his face and mine. It's not like we could whisper sweet nothings to each other, you know.

"Hello! Kind of chilly, isn't it?!" I'd holler, and he'd hurriedly wrap me up in his hand, ashamed he hadn't noticed... But his hand nearly squished me.

"Sorry," he mumbled, blushing a bit, then, more confidently, he said "Oh, I know!" and he turned to face me, opened his mouth and with a roar spit out a ball of fire. He almost burnt me to a crisp. He went all sad and embarrassed on me, lowered his eyes, hung his head, and curled his tail into a little ball. So I turned to him and shouted at the top of my lungs, "It's all right! I understand!" He felt so ashamed. He was such a late bloomer and our dates were always so platonic. But then one day—we'd been talking about family, where we grew up, whatever was on our minds, and then there was a lull in the conversation—he stuck his palm out, urged me to climb up, and brought me right up to his mouth... It was our first kiss. It had a radioactive taste.

Ever since I was a kid, I've always wanted to be an angel. I mean a real angel, not just somebody who looks like one. Not some god you have to believe in to be saved, and not a human being, someone who looks kind but is really just indecisive. I wanted to be somebody who takes it all in her stride—anger, sadness, loneliness, hatred, *everything*—and smiles right back at them without saying a word. Someone who is gentler than spring, with a heart bigger than summer, lovelier than autumn, and purer than winter—bathed in a harmonious light, warmer than that sun in the sky...

I'd like you to meet my father. I'm sure my mother will understand, and grandma and my sisters, they ought to be happy for me. But, my dad...my dad, he's very stubborn and old-fashioned. I'm sure he'll be against anybody I bring home. Probably won't even listen to me, or even agree to meet you. But, you know, he's really a very gentle daddy at heart. If we're really sincere, I'm sure he'll understand. So...Godzilla, let's go down the mountain! Let's go into town together. Come meet my dad!

Scene Two
The Journey

NARRATOR: November 21, 1986, 16:00 hours. Mt. Mihara's violent eruption had subsided for the time being. An eerie silence fell. Something else was about to happen—everyone at the meteorological observatory on the island of Oshima knew it. 16:15: white steam rose from the volcano's caldera, hovering over a point between the Yoroibata and Kengamine peaks. The steam turned into a plume of black smoke and then, suddenly, into red-hot lava. 16:27: the earth split open. The tower of smoke kept growing and the police called for everyone to evacuate. Even the daredevil reporters were forced to retreat, step by step. Black smoke threw a pall over the advancing evening, swallowing up the frantic evacuees, one by one—a veritable picture of hell at the last judgement.

It was the first time in twelve years that Mt. Mihara was active. It could explode anytime. The authorities at the Oshima observatory confirmed the potential for widespread destruction and they appealed to the governor of Tokyo to order all island residents to evacuate. But then, what's this? The boiling clouds parted and this young woman, who dreamt of becoming an angel, appeared out of the black smoke with…Godzilla!

YAYOI: More to the right! That's where my old school is, put your right foot there! And your left foot—there's a ranch beside that red roof, there! Watch the cows! And don't drag your tail! Hold the tip in your hand, like this—that's right. Don't spit fire! What's that? A cedar tree got stuck in your toes? You okay? We're almost there! Can you see it? That two-story house with the blue tile roof is my home. That's my room there, with the light blue curtains! Now, let me have a look at you. Well dressed, shoes polished, clean-shaven…right. Now, my father, Godzilla—make sure you greet him properly.

NARRATOR: Is it love, or an illusion? What will become of them? Where is this girl leading Godzilla? What is awaiting her?

Godzilla—offspring of mankind's meddling with nature—but look at his eyes, how gentle! They are gentler than a virgin's eyes, weeping over a solitary flower blossoming in the meadow.

Scene Three
Family

> *The Ichinose household. The dry clack of a water clapper and the sound of flowing water.*[*] *The family*

---
*water clapper (*shishiodoshi*): a bamboo tube on a pivot which, when filled with water from a pipe, tips and strikes a hard object like a stone, making a pleasing sound. Originally used as a kind of scarecrow in the fields, here it is merely an accessory for an elegant tea garden.

are going through the motions of practising the tea ceremony, portraying a formal marriage proposal.

TWIN 1: *(Imitating YAYOI's suitor.)* Mr. Ichinose, sir. I ask you for Yayoi's hand.

TWIN 2: *(Imitating YAYOI.)* Daddy, I want to marry him!

FATHER silently continues making tea.

TWIN 1: Sir, please!

TWIN 2: *(Still getting no reply.)* Daddy!

MOTHER: ...Honey...

FATHER: ...The birds are making quite a racket today, aren't they, mother?

MOTHER: Couldn't you just hear them out, dear?

FATHER: I'm making tea. The Ichinose School of Tea, an offshoot of the Urasenke School. A truly sensitive sort of tea ceremony—why, even the sounds of leaves rustling in the spring breeze makes me lose my concentration. Put out some birdfeed, would you, mother? That ought to shut them up for a while. Once their bellies are full, surely they'll fly back to their nests and give me a moment of peace. *(Silently continues making tea.)*

MOTHER: Honey...

TWIN 1: Mr. Ichinose, we're in love.

TWIN 2: Daddy, I love him!

FATHER: What are you waiting for, Mother? I'm not suggesting you shoot the birds and serve them for dinner tonight. No, what I'm saying is, fill their little bellies and send them back to their nests.

TWIN 2: Daddy, couldn't you *please* just listen to us?

FATHER: Shaddup! Tell them, mother, what I told you:

	I'll be the one who picks out the man my daughter will marry! Somebody who stands out and fits in. My eyes, my ears, my nose and, yeah, even the strength of this arm will do the picking!
MOTHER:	*(To TWINS.)* Maybe we ought to call it a day…
FATHER:	Do you remember, mother? When Yayoi was born we were quite poor and this bowl cost us a small fortune. We bought it for her, remember? We polished it carefully every day, making sure it didn't get even the slightest crack, waiting till her wedding day… We can't just let go of that bowl, can we, mother? Not till she brings us some fine young man who can build her a home, somebody who's worthy to follow in the steps of the Urasenke Ichinose School—till then we'll guard that bowl, or die trying!
GRANDMOTHER:	Bravo! Well said. *(Applause.)*
MOTHER:	I didn't think you had it in you, honey!
TWIN 1:	Way to go, Daddy!
TWIN 2:	Yeah!
GRANDMOTHER:	That's my son. Finally, all my hard work raising this boy is paying off. "Not till she brings us some fine young man who can build her a home, somebody who's worthy to follow in the steps of the Urasenke Ichinose School." …That'll put the fear of God in 'em. I don't care how ambitious the young man is, he'd think twice before crossing this door, and if he were some office boy, fresh out of college, I bet you he'd run off yelping with his tail between his legs.
ALL:	*(Praising him.)* Bravo! Bravo!

Blushing with embarrassment from their praise, FATHER struggles to find whatever way he can to regain paternal authority.

GRANDMOTHER: …However, I would like to offer some constructive criticism, if you don't mind. *(She lines up three teacups.)* So, what's this?

FATHER: *Bancha.*

GRANDMOTHER: It's black tea. What about this one?

FATHER: Roasted tea.

GRANDMOTHER: Coffee. And this one?

FATHER: Oolong tea.

GRANDMOTHER: Oolong my ass. It's Gatorade! *(Slaps him.)*

TWIN 1: I knew it!

TWIN 2: I got all worked up for nothing!

GRANDMOTHER: See? You'll never pull it off. All you've ever tasted is *bancha* and cheap roasted tea, supermarket stuff, or spiked oolong. You being some kind of tea master is way too much of a stretch. And look at the cheap bowl you're using! With Doraemon the cartoon cat on it! Who the hell are you fooling with that?

FATHER: S-sorry, we didn't have any proper tea bowls, mother. But Yayoi used to love that bowl when she was a kid, even if it wasn't so fancy. We've got to inject some realism into this scene.

GRANDMOTHER: Who gives a shit about realism! Ah, why did your father—God rest his soul!—suffer so to put you through college? I'm ashamed of you.

MOTHER: I've tried to tell him. But he won't listen. He's stubborn, isn't he?

GRANDMOTHER: His stubbornness is not the issue. You ought to anticipate what he might say or do to shame this

	family—you should put a bee in his ear before he goes and disgraces us in public. That's the duty of a good wife.
TWIN 2:	Mummy, can we be excused now?
TWIN 1:	I can't stand this anymore. Let's go out and play.
GRANDMOTHER:	Hold it, you two. Listen up. You're in the last year of your compulsory education. Next year, you two twins will turn into bashful high school co-eds. You'll be trained in our ancient Japanese customs to be proper young ladies—besides, you ought to know by now that this bowl doesn't cut the mustard. Understand?
TWINS:	*(Together.)* Nope.
GRANDMOTHER:	Don't say "nope" in unison like that.
MOTHER:	Mother, forget it. It's not going to work.
FATHER:	Right. Who do we think we are? I went to work for the company fresh out of college, married one of girls in the office. And here we are, with three kids living in a three-room pre-fab with walls full of cracks, thirty years left on the mortgage and a family vacation once a year I pay for by skimping on smokes. ...Who the hell are we to complain about our future son-in-law!
GRANDMOTHER:	Weakling. This is like a, what do you call it? A formality. They'll be worse off if everybody supported them from the get-go. Can't you see their love will be much stronger if they've got to jump a few hurdles first? Let's show them what real love is, challenge them heart and soul. Then they can go on to savour the hard-won compromises and complacency of married life.
MOTHER:	Mother, I don't mean to disagree with you, but shouldn't we just quietly deal with those hurdles you're talking about without making a big deal?

	We could say instead there's something wrong with his family name, or his house faces an unlucky direction.
FATHER:	Or we could object to his religion, or where he was born—Chiba, Saitama, Gunma, and Ibaragi are absolutely out of the question.*
GRANDMOTHER:	Where's the drama, then? You gotta have drama.
TWIN 2:	You're going to say yes in the end, so why bother making such a fuss?
TWIN 1:	Yeah! If you give Yayoi and her boyfriend a really hard time now, what'll happen when it's our turn?
GRANDMOTHER:	Well, when it's your turn, the men will have to duke it out.
TWIN 2:	Get serious. If that's the deal, we can only bring home pro wrestlers!
FATHER:	So, it's okay if I get beaten to a pulp? No fair! Why pick on your dear old dad? This isn't supposed to be about winning or losing.
TWIN 1:	Hey, you can't make an omelette without breaking a few eggs. What happens to us, daddy, if our boyfriends run off snivelling, covered in blood?
GRANDMOTHER:	What would you do with wimps like that anyway?
MOTHER:	Grandma, the girls are right. Not many young men today have the guts for a fight.
TWIN 1:	I'm not marrying a *yakuza* gangster—no way!
FATHER:	Stop talking about gangsters and pro wrestlers!
GRANDMOTHER:	Bring 'em on! I'm ready for 'em!
FATHER:	Mother, I'm begging you—please, give it a rest!

*Chiba, Saitama, Gunma and Ibaragi: these are all prefectures around the perimeter of the metropolitan Toyko area, bedroom communities within commuting distance that are hardly fashionable places to live.

TWIN 2:	That's why you should give the new boy a little trouble, just for the sake of form. Make him visit a couple of times to test his true intentions.
TWIN 1:	Precisely.
MOTHER:	What do you say, Dad?
FATHER:	Well, since this is our first time and I've got two more daughters to spare, let's go along with it. We'll consider it a warm-up…

Scene Four
Hayata's Heartbreak

HAYATA:	(*Entering suddenly from his hiding spot.*) A warm-up, Mr. Ichinose?
FATHER:	Oh, Hatchan!
MOTHER:	Oh, my God, Hatchan, when did you get here?
HAYATA:	I'll admit I'm feeling a wee bit guilty about playing hookey from my sacred duty as Motomachi's cop on the beat, especially to break into your house to eavesdrop. But this here "warm up," Mr. Ichinose—I can't allow it.
TWIN 2:	Oh God, it's him!
TWIN 1:	Yeah, now there's really going to be a bloodbath.
HAYATA:	If you've gotta play, then play to win!
FATHER:	We were going to tell you. Look, this happened all very suddenly.
MOTHER:	That's right. Yayoi just told us on the phone. She said, "There's someone I want you to meet. I'm bringing him over." I haven't the slightest idea what she meant.

HAYATA:	Well, I don't need to ask, but surely you're going to say no!
FATHER:	You will say no, right, Mother?
MOTHER:	Yes, yes, of course. I'm sure she'll marry you, Hatchan—what on earth was she thinking?
FATHER:	Maybe she took a knock on the head and lost her memory or something. Not to worry, Hatchan.
GRANDMOTHER:	Didn't you say, Tsumugi, we're all worthless and our house is falling to bits, so this family shouldn't be so choosy about a son-in-law?
FATHER:	Maybe this isn't the time to be picking on your daughter-in-law, Mother.
GRANDMOTHER:	You poor thing, Hatchan—ever since you were little, dreaming of the day you'd marry this sweet girl. Why, you even got "I Love Yayoi" tattooed on your arm. She'll pay for this!
FATHER:	Mother, we don't even know what kind of man she might bring home. Nothing's been decided yet.
MOTHER:	That's right Mr. Hayata, we're not so dumb as to give our daughter away to just anybody.
GRANDMOTHER:	What if he's a Tokyo University grad?
TWINS:	Really?!
FATHER:	Well, there's all kinds, even at Tokyo U. Academic background ain't everything…
GRANDMOTHER:	How about somebody from Sony?
TWINS:	Cool!
MOTHER:	Well, there's nothing wrong with a good salary, but…
GRANDMOTHER:	Anyway, it's got to be higher than a cop's salary in

	Oshima Motomachi. How about this: the second son of some big business tycoon. "You have only daughters, so how about an adopted son-in-law to carry on your name?"*
TWINS:	Awesome!
MOTHER:	If we adopt a son-in-law we'll get a dowry, won't we?*
FATHER:	We can expect better than that from our new relatives. They might be a bit sarcastic at first, saying "I can't see how our son can fit in your home," but since we're all family now they'll eventually come round and say, "We've bought a new house, we'd be pleased if you use it."
TWIN 1:	If they've got a big company, I'm sure they've got another son to spare.
TWIN 2:	Hey, unfair. What about me?
TWIN 1:	Don't worry—he'll introduce a friend to you.
HAYATA:	*(While on the telephone, he pulls out his gun.)* Ah, hello Chief? Hayata here. Seems I dropped my gun somewhere. Right, it's got six bullets. File a report for me, would you? Let's hope some bad guy doesn't find it, eh? Ha, ha, ha…click. *(Hangs up the phone.)*
FATHER:	Your gun? Why, Hayata, isn't that—
HAYATA:	*(Training his gun on the family, in a last ditch effort, he states his case.)* Strolling up the mountain together, her smile playing hide-and-seek in the sunlight through the trees overhead, a smile so dazzling that I have to suddenly stop and squint. The wind off the sea blows her hair, and the way she brushes that stray lock from her cheek is adorable. I grab her by the shoulders and embrace her. "I love how

---

*adopted son-in-law (*yôshi*): in Japan, families with only daughters will often adopt a son through marriage to ensure that the family name is preserved.

the sea always sparkles so!" she whispers. I can still hear her voice. She wouldn't shed a single tear if somebody tried to harm her and she'd keep smiling if anybody betrayed her. And I vowed to those lips with that inextinguishable smile that if I was born for one task it was to protect her. Some guy tried to chat her up, so I flipped him over my back and tossed him into the sea. Somebody crossed her path and made eyes at her, so I booted him clear over Mt. Mihara. The cops caught me every time, so what could I do but become a cop myself?

FATHER: I...I know how you feel—I really do.

MOTHER: Listen, let's stop this nonsense. We understand, okay?

HAYATA: Can't wait to see the morning paper: "Family massacred in Oshima Motomachi with cop's revolver—work of a madman?"

TWIN 2: Hang on there. "Family massacre"? You're not talking about us.

TWIN 1: I don't want to die with you guys, no way!

HAYATA: Who raised you girls? Yayoi was brought up pure as the driven snow, so what in the world happened to you two? You should be like your sister!

TWINS: Get serious.

TWIN 2: She's so star-eyed...

TWIN 1: Dorky-dressed...

TWIN 2: Make-up-less...

TWIN 1: Goody-goody...

TWIN 2: Out of it...

TWIN 1: Clueless...

TWIN 2: Uncool...

TWINS: Total loser!

HAYATA: Enough already! Mocking her in stereo, for Crissake! I'll start by killing the two of you.

GRANDMOTHER: Now, now Hatchan, there's plenty of time for that. You should check out your rival first.

HAYATA: Yeah, but he's a Tokyo University grad. Works for Sony, some rich kid, right?

GRANDMOTHER: Those were just examples!

MOTHER, FATHER, TWINS: Whaaaaaat?

HAYATA: I hate all of you!

REPORTER: We're here in Oshima Motomachi. Godzilla has suddenly appeared on Mt. Mihara and is slowly advancing this way, but it would seem for some reason he's carefully avoiding people's homes and other buildings, as if somebody were guiding him. So, to this point it looks like there's not been much damage, but it won't stay that way once he enters the port. Most of the islanders have left; the last of them have boarded the rescue ship Katori and are about to sail away!

HAYATA: Who the hell are you?

REPORTER: What are you people doing here?

TWIN 1: Hey, what's all this about Godzilla?

HAYATA: Oh yeah, I completely forgot! This is no time to quarrel—Godzilla's heading our way! Where's Yayoi? Where did she go?

FATHER: G-Godzilla? You mean, *the* Godzilla?

REPORTER:	Haven't you heard? Don't you people watch the news? Godzilla's coming!
MOTHER:	Uh, Dad, what'll we do?
FATHER:	Right, now, uh, let's not lose our heads. Grab what you can and run!

The family panics.

GRANDMOTHER:	So, he's finally come…
REPORTER:	You say "finally." D'you know something, Grannie?
GRANDMOTHER:	Three years ago, Godzilla was lured up to the mouth of the volcano—he should've died there, but…
FATHER:	Nobody gives a shit about that now, Mother. We have to get out of here. Everybody!
HAYATA:	Whoa! Hang on just a minute. Where's Yayoi?
FATHER:	Don't know. She should be on her way.
TWIN 2:	Let's get the hell out of here!
MOTHER:	I bet you Yayoi's heading for the port. We can meet her there!
HAYATA:	You're just trying to save yourselves, and there's no way I'm going to let you! No one leaves this house till we find her!
REPORTER:	Look at this, folks! A breath-taking drama is about to unfold here on Oshima, this ordinary tourist destination. Godzilla's just a few hundred meters away but, concerned for the safety of the woman he loves, this perfectly ordinary Oshima policeman has turned into a man obsessed, waving his revolver and holding her family hostage. Thank God that I'm here to witness this. Godzilla may step on me, Godzilla may even eat me, but I'll carry

	out my duty as a news reporter to the end!
HAYATA:	Hold on! Who's obsessed??
REPORTER:	W-what I mean to say is, the story's more entertaining that way.
HAYATA:	Okay, let's make it even more entertaining then. We'll start with you!
REPORTER:	H-help!

Scene Five
Yayoi's Home/The Boyfriend

YAYOI:	I'm back!
ALL:	...Yayoi!
YAYOI:	Why, Mr. Hayata, you're here too?
HAYATA:	What do you mean by that? Where the hell did you go? Come on, let's get out of here.
YAYOI:	Daddy, I've brought someone over I'd like you to meet.
FATHER:	This isn't exactly the time for that. We've got to get out of here!
TWINS:	Come on, Yayoi. Hurry!
REPORTER:	That's it, it's all over. He's practically on top of us.
	FATHER, MOTHER, TWINS and HAYATA panic.
YAYOI:	Come on in! It's okay.
FATHER:	Okay? Yayoi, not now!
GODZILLA:	*(Entering; scrunching noises underfoot.)* Good evening, everybody.

FATHER, MOTHER, TWINS, REPORTER, HAYATA:	Aaaaahh!!
YAYOI:	Let me introduce you. Daddy, this is Mr. Godzilla.
FATHER:	Introduce me? Wha…?
TWIN 1:	Yayoi's new boyfriend…
FATHER, MOTHER, HAYATA, TWINS, REPORTER:	Godzilla!!
GODZILLA:	Pleased to meet you.
REPORTER:	Ladies and gentlemen, this is incredible! There's never been anything like this in the whole history of mankind. It's brilliant!
HAYATA:	Brilliant? H-hey you, Godzilla! W-what do you want?
GODZILLA:	So pleased to meet you. You are…?
HAYATA:	Whoa! Back off there! Are you trying to crush me?
GODZILLA:	Whoops! Sorry!
HAYATA:	I-I'm Yayoi's fiancé. You got that?
YAYOI:	He's an old friend, looked out for me ever since we were kids.
HAYATA:	Yayoi, what were you thinking, bringing this creature here? *(To GODZILLA.)* You, you forced yourself on her, didn't you? I'm not going to let you get away with this! Never!
FATHER:	Whoa there, Hayata.

GODZILLA: You must be Yayoi's father. I'm really so pleased to meet you. I'm Godzilla.

FATHER: I know, already! Just don't come any closer.

GODZILLA: (*Backs up.*) Sorry.

MOTHER: Yikes! Look out! Watch the foot, the right foot!

             (*Crunching sounds.*) Oh my God, it's Itô's place next door—flat as a pancake.

YAYOI: Please be careful. We must go over together later to apologize.

FATHER: Come over here a sec, Yayoi, would you please?

MOTHER: Quietly, so he doesn't notice.

FATHER: Hatchan, do something to distract Godzilla for a moment.

HAYATA: Roger! Hey, Godzilla! (*Distracts GODZILLA.*)

MOTHER: Now!

FATHER: (*Wrenching YAYOI away.*) Yayoi! Are you hurt?

YAYOI: Hurt? Daddy...

MOTHER: You must've had the fright of your life. It's all right now, you're here with us.

YAYOI: Mummy...

HAYATA: Right, Yayoi, let's get the hell out of here.

YAYOI: Just a minute, please!

FATHER: Right now, everybody, let's clear out!

MOTHER: Where's Grannie, dear?...

TWIN 2:   Seems she made a break for it again.

TWIN 1:   Now, isn't that just like her!

TWINS:	Who gives a shit? Let's get out of here!
HAYATA:	Hurry!
GODZILLA:	*Gaaaooo! (Roars; the sound of flames.)*
ALL:	Aaaaahh!!
YAYOI:	Don't frighten them! You know that's not nice.
GODZILLA:	Sorry. But they're not really listening to what you're saying.
YAYOI:	Please everybody, he means well. Don't leave.
TWIN 2:	You've really lost it, Yayoi.
TWIN 1:	Where's your Sony man, the tycoon's son and his very good-looking friend?
FATHER:	Yayoi, you must have taken a knock on the head.
MOTHER:	You're not serious are you, Yayoi?
REPORTER:	Sorry to butt in here, folks, but could you liven it up a bit? This is a once-in-a-lifetime event we're experiencing. I mean, listen to yourselves. Couldn't you possibly say something a bit more significant, more interesting? Godzilla himself is here, and the whole world's watching.
HAYATA:	*(To REPORTER.)* Oh, I see. You want is something interesting? Then, shut up! Godzilla! Big reporter here has ratings to consider. Why, I bet you're really hungry. Looks tasty, don't you think? Go ahead, eat! Now that's breaking news, eh? "What's in Godzilla's stomach? Tonight at eleven." *(To REPORTER.)* You'll get the Pulitzer Prize. Have a nice trip!
REPORTER:	No thanks!
YAYOI:	Mr. Hayata, we've already had our dinner.
MOTHER:	Y-Yayoi. Both your arms and legs look okay…

FATHER:	What part got eaten, then? You're daddy's little girl, you have to tell us. Be honest now, I won't get angry.
HAYATA:	You beast, you! What have you done? Spit it out! Here! Right now!
YAYOI:	I'm all right. You think he ate me?
REPORTER:	So, what *was* for dinner…?
YAYOI:	We stopped at a ranch on the way over—there was this cow… But we left some cash.
REPORTER:	And what did *you* have?
YAYOI:	You wouldn't believe how sweet he is. He tore off the choicest morsel for me, fired up his breath and cooked it on the spot—nice and rare. It was delicious. Wasn't it, Godzilla?
GODZILLA:	Yummy.
REPORTER:	Do you see that, folks? Smiling maiden, born in this till now unremarkable place, Oshima Motomachi, tames long-standing enemy of the human race, Godzilla. Why, he's practically a pussy cat! We'll build a new home for this girl and her Godzilla on a hill overlooking the Pacific Ocean. Who needs a Security Pact with the U.S. or the Self Defence Forces? Not Japan, not anymore. Who cares about their nukes? Who gives a damn about trade friction? Japan no longer has anything to fear.
YAYOI:	I didn't tame him like some beast. We're in love!
TWIN 2:	Yayoi, you've gone a wee bit overboard, haven't you?
TWIN 1:	You oughta be like us, Yayoi, and cut loose every once in a while. You can always get back on the straight and narrow when you want to.

TWIN 2:	So you think you're above us all, eh? Just standing there next to Mr.'Zilla, saying "we're in *love*!"
TWIN 1:	It's not normal, you know.
TWIN 2:	I know just the guy for you, Yayoi.
TWIN 1:	If you go in for the strong type, we'll get you a gangster or a pro wrestler or something.
TWIN 2:	Somebody better than Godzilla.
YAYOI:	Emi and Yumi, listen. I really am in love with him.
TWINS:	Uh uh! Godzilla as our brother—no way!
FATHER:	Shaddup! Love? Don't make me laugh. *(To GODZILLA.)* And as for you, I'll be the one who picks out the man my daughter will marry! Somebody who stands out and fits in. My eyes, my ears, my nose and, yeah, even the strength of this arm will do the picking! Why, you pipsqueak, you…you little twit!…
MOTHER:	He seems quite strong, honey. I wouldn't mess with him.
FATHER:	SHADDUP!!
HAYATA:	Easy does it, dad! You look a bit shaky on your feet.
REPORTER:	Anyway, Mr. Ichinose, let's hear from *him*.
HAYATA:	Hear from him? What could he possibly say?
REPORTER:	Well, how they fell in love, for example.
HAYATA:	Fell in love? Just what do you mean by that?
REPORTER:	Like, they met at school or something.
HAYATA:	Godzilla goes to school? Don't make me laugh.
REPORTER:	Maybe she was walking in town, and he was lost and asked for directions.

HAYATA:	Before he'd finished asking, they'd have called in the army.
YAYOI:	We met on the mountain. Hiding far from men's eyes he'd turned to stone. A violet bloomed there, on his body; I climbed up close to see. Just then…

Scene Six
The Mountaintop (Boy Meets Girl)

The mountaintop. Covered in vegetation and mistaken for a boulder, GODZILLA senses the girl's presence and is aroused from his long slumber.

GODZILLA:	Hi.
YAYOI:	Hi.
GODZILLA:	I'm terribly sorry. I must've startled you.
YAYOI:	Not at all. What are you doing here?
GODZILLA:	I was sleeping.
YAYOI:	I'm terribly sorry. I woke you, didn't I?
GODZILLA:	That's okay. I was tired of sleeping.
YAYOI:	How long were you asleep?
GODZILLA:	About three years, I guess. (*Pause.*) You're not afraid?
YAYOI:	Of what?
GODZILLA:	Why, of me.
YAYOI:	Not at all. Should I be?
GODZILLA:	People take one look at me and run.
YAYOI:	…Um, could you lower yourself a bit? I'm not scared.

GODZILLA: Uh, okay.

YAYOI: Maybe...

GODZILLA: Maybe what?

YAYOI: It must've been your eyes—they looked so gentle.

GODZILLA: Now, you're embarrassing me. ...*Gaaoo!* (*Breathes fire.*) Oh, dear, I'm terribly sorry. I didn't burn you, did I?

YAYOI: I'm all right. (*Giggles shyly.*)

GODZILLA: Is something funny?

YAYOI: It's so cute.

GODZILLA: What?

YAYOI: The violet, in your tail.

GODZILLA: Oh, uh, yes.

YAYOI: I love violets. Mind you don't crush it.

GODZILLA: Certainly not!

YAYOI: My name's Yayoi Ichinose. And you are...?

GODZILLA: Pardon me, I should've introduced myself. I'm Godzilla. *Gaaaooo!* (*Breathes out fire.*)

Scene Seven
Back to Life

Back at the Ichinose household.

ALL: Aaaaahh!

HAYATA: Careful with the fire! Watch the fire, please!

GODZILLA: So sorry!

YAYOI: He's really a very nice person, Daddy.

HAYATA: He's not a person!

REPORTER: Now, calm down, everyone. Godzilla shows no sign that he means any harm—look, he's opened his heart to you people. So why not try and talk to him?

HAYATA: Why can't you just shut up?

FATHER: Okay, Yayoi, let's say you're in love, then. Where do you expect this to go? I mean, what kind of future…?

GODZILLA: Mr. Ichinose, I want to marry her.

FATHER: You know, not that I care, but, there, under your knee…

GODZILLA: What?

FATHER: Under your knee. …That's our car, traded up just last year—flat as a tin sheet.

MOTHER: Sorry if I'm harping on this, but surely you're not serious, Yayoi.

YAYOI: We've been going out together for a while now, and we're thinking of getting married.

FATHER: Marry Godzilla? Just what planet is my daughter from?

TWIN 2: Yayoi, no matter how naïve you are, surely you understand what it means to get married, don't you?

TWIN 1: No way. Her naïveté is in a whole different dimension altogether.

YAYOI: Of course, I know. Marriage is…

ALL: Yes?!

YAYOI: Marriage is a vow of true love till death do us part.

An absurd silence.

HAYATA: I love you, Yayoi! I knew it! That's my girl. Now I *know* it wasn't a mistake to save myself for her.

REPORTER: Ladies and gentlemen, am I the only one to hear it? That voice—the still small voice, so to speak, of an angel—a smile on her lips, professing the very words we in our barren hearts have forgotten? Our hearts have been as cold as stone, but we now stand stunned, mouths agape—

GODZILLA: *(To FATHER.)* Sir.

FATHER: Excuse me?

GODZILLA: Please give me Yayoi's hand. I'll make her very happy. I promise!

FATHER: Uh, sure, be my guest!

ALL: Daddy!

FATHER: *(Catching himself.)* I mean, no way!

MOTHER: Listen, you! If you're getting married there's got to be a wedding, right? It's a once-in-a-lifetime event for a girl: there, before her all her family and friends, she and her man make a vow to God to be husband and wife.

GODZILLA: I'm non-sectarian, so shrine or church, either's fine with me.

MOTHER: That's not the point! What I mean is, *all* our relatives have to be there: my family, his brothers and sisters, grandparents, everybody. Then, of course, we have to invite the same number from your family to even things out.

GODZILLA: So, that's what you meant? No problem, then—I've got lots of brothers and sisters too, Mrs. Ichinose.

	There's Gappa, and Gamera, and Radon…
MOTHER:	No problem? Oh, yes there is! Don't you get it? When all your monster family and friends show up, Russia, America, they're not going to take it lying down. They'll be shooting off missiles to congratulate you.
GODZILLA:	Missiles never scared us any.
MOTHER:	Fine for you, but what about us? What about us, huh?
YAYOI:	I'll appeal to Mr. Reagan and Mr. Gorbachev, mummy.
MOTHER:	I really do hope you're joking, 'cause I don't want to think I made a mistake in how I brought you up.
FATHER:	And what about the wedding hall? There really isn't any place that can fit all your relatives. Just ten of you guys could fill Yokohama Stadium.
YAYOI:	Listen, Daddy, how about where Godzilla and I used to date—Mt. Mihara? We could put fifty or sixty creatures up there…
FATHER:	You're missing the point, Yayoi. What I mean is, ordinarily folk don't hold weddings in places like Yokohama Stadium or Mt. Mihara.
YAYOI:	Yes, what if it rained? My wedding dress would get soaked.
FATHER:	I don't mean that either. We'll sort that out later…
HAYATA:	For crissake, Mr. Ichinose. Let me deal with this!
MOTHER & TWINS:	Go for it!
REPORTER:	We've got a substitute player, folks. Officer Hayata, from Oshima Motomachi Precinct—that's Yayoi Ichinose's fiancé. What's his plan?

HAYATA:	Yayoi, can we talk? Please calm down—let's think this over.
YAYOI:	Certainly!
HAYATA:	You described the meaning of marriage just perfectly a short while ago—a totally sentimental world, so common everyone's forgotten what it means. They're all concerned with more serious issues, like the origin of species...
GODZILLA:	You mean, Darwin?
HAYATA:	Don't show off, Godzilla!
YAYOI:	He's very bright, you know!
HAYATA:	I know, I know. Godzilla's a genius. But what about you, Yayoi? What about children?
REPORTER:	A sneak attack, ladies and gentlemen. He's gone for the jugular...
YAYOI:	Children...
YAYOI & TWINS:	The stork brings them.
TWIN 2:	That's what you think.
REPORTER:	Nice dodge!
GODZILLA:	Where I come from, Radon brings them.
HAYATA:	You're making fun of us, right?
FATHER:	Listen, Yayoi's our eldest daughter. We'll be in trouble if she can't bring home a son-in-law and healthy grandkids to keep the Ichinose family going. We've got to protect our name, you see.
GODZILLA:	Leave it to me, I'll protect you! Who's the enemy? King Ghidorah? Alien Valtan?*

*King Ghidorah: a three-headed monster that appeared in *Ghidorah* (1964) and several other Godzilla sequels. Alien Valtan: a monster from the 1960s television series, *Ultraman*.

FATHER:	You're missing the point again. Why would King Ghidorah or Alien Valtan attack an ordinary family like ours?
YAYOI:	Daddy, he says he's okay with being an adopted son.
GODZILLA:	You see, I don't have a family name to carry on.
HAYATA:	Godzilla hasn't got a family name? Of course not.
YAYOI:	Daddy, I love Godzilla. But I'd still love him even if he weren't a Godzilla. Even if he happened to be, say, a snake, a panda, or a slug.
REPORTER:	Tense moment here, folks. Mum and Dad's hearts are pounding.
FATHER:	Your dad was such a romantic in the old days. I'm a real sucker for sincerity.
MOTHER:	A slug, you say. Well, who's to say we're not better off after all. …
TWINS & HAYATA:	Worse!
HAYATA:	Yayoi, please think this over. Even as we speak, Japan's at loggerheads with the rest of the world over trade friction. Were Godzilla to marry a Japanese girl on top of that, think of the military threat…
TWIN 2:	That ain't gonna work—you'll have to do better than that.
TWIN 1:	She's totally got flowers for brains.
HAYATA:	Yayoi, don't you read the papers?
YAYOI:	No, they get my hands dirty…
REPORTER:	Yayoi, don't you watch TV?
YAYOI:	Uh uh, it makes my heart dirty.

Scene Eight
Tadpole

The stage is suddenly transformed as if into the ocean, or a sky filled with twinkling stars. GRANDMOTHER appears, beautiful, like a screen actress from days gone by.

GRANDMOTHER: No, they get my hands dirty! ...Uh uh, it makes my heart dirty!

YAYOI: Grandma!!

GRANDMOTHER: Look, Yayoi. What can the sea, lit up by the sun with the light of a million candles, what can it show you?

YAYOI: Tens of millions of dazzling jewels!

GRANDMOTHER: And look, Yayoi. What can the stars, studding a night sky that gently lulls people to sleep, what can they offer you?

YAYOI: Sweet happiness and humble love! What's that, Grandma? What's everybody looking at? They seem so happy.

GRANDMOTHER: It's called television. An infernal machine that pollutes the heart.

YAYOI: And why are they laughing, Grandma?

GRANDMOTHER: What the hell are you watching? Channel 8?

YAYOI: And what are they saying?

GRANDMOTHER: Close your eyes, Yayoi. One glance at Fuji Sankei will turn you into a twit! Don't be fooled by them, Yayoi. Go talk to the flowers in the field. Go listen to the whisper of the breezes sighing in the trees. Just like your beautiful, pure and undefiled grandma, who all her life kept her eyes on love.

GODZILLA: Excuse me.

GRANDMOTHER: What is it?

YAYOI: Allow me to introduce him, Grandma. This is Godzilla.

GODZILLA: Pleased to meet you.

GRANDMOTHER: I know who it is! What I want to know is, why is he here?

YAYOI: I want to spend my life with him.

GODZILLA: Forgive my lack of social graces, but I'm happy to meet you.

GRANDMOTHER: Lack of social graces? That's putting it mildly!

YAYOI: Grandma…

GRANDMOTHER: Yayoi, come over here.

YAYOI: Okay.

GRANDMOTHER: Your grandma's pretty progressive, you know, so I don't have an axe to grind about his not being human. Still…

GODZILLA: Thank you. Just knowing there's even one of you who'll say that gives us courage.

YAYOI: That's great, isn't it, Godzilla? Thanks, Grandma.

GRANDMOTHER: What have I got to hide? My first love was a tadpole.

FATHER: A what? That's news to me!

MOTHER: Darling, you never told me your dad was a tadpole!

GRANDMOTHER: It was a love so intense that just thinking about it now makes me feel hot all over. I used to sneak out at night to meet him, right under my parents' noses. I'd stand at the edge of the pond. I'd look in and he'd look out—we'd look at each other—we didn't need words at all. When one night, under a sky just brimming with stars, I discovered two little hands sprouting from his body, I could've jumped with joy. I was just a bashful nineteen-year-old virgin, but I stuck my finger into the water and he gently caressed its tip. We prayed to God: "Please, God! We beg you! Change him into a person, not a frog! That's all we ask for!"

REPORTER: Well, was your prayer heard?

GRANDMOTHER: It was hopeless, from the start. His hands and feet had…webs.

YAYOI: Poor Grandma…

GRANDMOTHER: Still, I thought I didn't mind. He lost his tail and grew up to be a splendid frog. I'd put him on my shoulder and run about the fields and climb the hills. I vowed to be faithful to this frog till death do us part. One day, he appeared by my pillow. I was sure he'd come to make love to me and I was ready to give myself to him. But…

YAYOI: But…?

GRANDMOTHER: He began to croak ever so sadly, then turned his back to me and stuck out his bum. I was so shocked I couldn't talk. He…was a she.

MOTHER: *(To FATHER.)* Lucky for you!

YAYOI: Grandma…

GRANDMOTHER: I cried my eyes out, for three whole days and nights. I'll never fall in love again, I thought. My first love—I was nineteen, a virgin—and it was spring, the month of April, and all the flowers were falling. Oh, April is the cruelest month!…

YAYOI: That's a beautiful story, grandma.

TWINS:	Yeah, right. *(Sarcastic.)* As if!
HAYATA:	That's my girl! I love you, Yayoi!
GRANDMOTHER:	It was a year later I met your father at a ranch in the mountains.
FATHER:	Don't tell me he was a bull, please!
GRANDMOTHER:	The bull's tail was covered in flies.
MOTHER:	Darling, your dad was a fly?
FATHER:	Give me a break, please. My father was a proper human being.
GRANDMOTHER:	Flies and I just didn't get along, you see—we didn't last a year. The one you thought was your father—he was my next husband.
YAYOI:	I know you, Grandma—you'll understand. I love him. I want to spend the rest of my life with him.
GODZILLA:	We beg of you. I promise to make her happy.
GRANDMOTHER:	It won't work.
YAYOI:	Why? Why won't it work?!
GRANDMOTHER:	Listen to me, Yayoi. He's already got a kid.
YAYOI:	What?
GRANDMOTHER:	Minilla!*
GODZILLA:	*(Kneels and hangs his head.)* Yayoi, I didn't mean to hide it from you. I was going to explain everything in front of your parents.
GRANDMOTHER:	Yayoi's my grandchild, you know. She's the apple of my eye. I've raised her far from all the filth that exists in this world, so how dare you saddle her with a hand-me-down kid? I won't have her suffer like that!

*Minilla (a.k.a. Minya): Godzilla's clumsy son appeared in *Son of Godzilla* (1967).

FATHER:	This is absurd! "Please, give me your daughter's hand." Aren't you the least bit ashamed? It's not even her own child, but a mini-Godzilla she'd have to raise! Go on, get out of here, back to Mt. Mihara or wherever you came from. Yayoi, pretend it was all a bad dream and forget about it.
YAYOI:	I'll raise it, even if it isn't mine. I know I can.
MOTHER:	It's no ordinary child. You'd have to climb a ladder to pat its head. And when it's naughty and you want to lock it in the closet, you'd have to build a gymnasium.
GRANDMOTHER:	You ought to know better than anybody else how much trouble Yayoi's in for if she marries you. If you really love her, wouldn't it be the manly thing to do—or rather the Godzilla-like thing to do—to leave now, without saying a word?
YAYOI:	Grandma, why don't you understand? What'll I do if you give up on me too?

During the following speech, GODZILLA slowly rises and spreads out his hands and becomes the fierce Godzilla, the monster everyone is afraid of.

GODZILLA:	It's true…I am Godzilla. It's true I have a child from a previous relationship. But this love for Yayoi is different…I know it's different. I won't give her up. *Gaaaoooo!* (*Breathes fire.*)
ALL:	Aaaahh!
HAYATA:	There, that's what you really are!
YAYOI:	You're wrong. He's…he's just a bit agitated. Isn't that right, Godzilla?
GODZILLA:	I, uh…*Gaaaaoo!* (*Breathes fire.*)
REPORTER:	This is a fine mess we're in, folks. Godzilla's been tamer than a pussy cat, but suddenly he's heard the

call of the wild—he's spitting fire at everybody in sight!

FATHER: I hope to God, Yayoi, you've figured it out by now. Godzilla can't help but be Godzilla.

MOTHER: It's a miracle, Yayoi, you haven't been burnt to a crisp.

YAYOI: He's not that kind of guy! Mummy, daddy, please understand!

GRANDMOTHER: I'll be damned if I'm going to let him trash my home like this. I'll show you!

*South sea rhythms. Suddenly the TWINS have become four inches tall and are standing on the palm of GRANDMOTHER's hand in an attitude of prayer, singing the "Mothra Song."**

REPORTER: Wh...what now!?

GRANDMOTHER: On your knees! Make way for our guardian deity, Lord Mothra!

GRANDMOTHER, FATHER, MOTHER, TWINS, HAYATA, REPORTER throw themselves down, their hands clasped in prayer.

Scene Nine

Brother worm

An enormous egg descends, out of which hatches a rather domesticated-looking MOTHRA. The family, HAYATA, and REPORTER back away from YAYOI and GODZILLA. The stage quickly becomes MOTHRA's home.

MOTHRA: Hey, brother, long time no see.

*Mothra Song: Appearing as tiny princesses to a giant moth larva, popular twin duo The Peanuts sang this song in the 1964 film *Mothra vs. Godzilla*. The lyrics (which are gibberish even in Japanese) run as follows: Mosura ya Mosura / dongan kasakuyan in dômu / rusutoritora hanba hanbamuyan / radabanuradan tonju kanraa / kasaku yaanmu.

GODZILLA: Hey, Mothra, you're looking good.

YAYOI: You're...brothers?

GODZILLA: Yes, same father, but different mothers.

MOTHRA: Who's the girl?

GODZILLA: Let me introduce you, Mo'. This is Yayoi Ichinose.

YAYOI: I'm pleased to meet you.

MOTHRA: And I'm pleased to meet you! I'm Mothra. What's up, brother, another movie? Last time, it was Yasuko Sawaguchi, but she's really not my type. Is she the new "star"?*

GODZILLA: Actually Mo', I'm thinking of, uh, getting married.

MOTHRA: Who with?

GODZILLA: Her.

MOTHRA: Who is?

GODZILLA: Me.

MOTHRA: ...Well, you look after yourself, brother. Got to run—I'm in the middle of a job.

GODZILLA: Mothy!

YAYOI: Mothra, I don't much care for tapeworms or earthworms, but I'm trying! I hope you understand!

MOTHRA: Listen, young lady, worms are worms and will remain so for the rest of their full but silly little lives. I'm a caterpillar. I may look like a *pain au chocolat* now—I'm still just a Mothra larva, after all—but I'll show you! One day soon I'll metamorphosize into a gorgeous imago!

YAYOI: Stupid me! I've upset you.

*Yasuko Sawaguchi made her debut as the leading lady in the 1984 remake of *Godzilla*, released in North America as *Godzilla 1985*.

MOTHRA: I can see you find me sickening, so forget about trying. Oh, how I hate getting older! Still, they idolized me once.

GODZILLA: Easy does it, Big Mo!

MOTHRA: What in hell's name were you thinking, brother?

GODZILLA: She's a really fine person, pretty and gentle.

MOTHRA: Even I can see that much. But she is not a Godzilla, with a sexy tail and a cute little muzzle spitting fire in pretty colours.

YAYOI: We love each other.

GODZILLA: That's right, Mothra.

MOTHRA: "That's right, Mothra." …Why, brother, must you always cause me such trouble? And your last movie—what was that? That "blockbuster" for Tôhô's fiftieth anniversary, the one with all the hype…?

YAYOI: (*Performing from the movie.*) "…But Mr. Defence Minister, with our current weapons, can we withstand Godzilla's heat rays?"

MOTHRA: "We can. Describe your defences."

GODZILLA: "Sir, it's a top-secret military aircraft built to protect the capital, extremely heat-resistant, armoured with titanium alloy and platinum circuitry… "

MOTHRA: "A veritable flying fortress—its name is Super X!"

GODZILLA & YAYOI: "Super X!!"

MOTHRA: Super X? You gotta be joking. Sounds like the name of some kinda cleanser.

GODZILLA: That's Super Suds!

YAYOI: Or the Super X discount store!

MOTHRA: Super X... Sheesh! Have you no shame? Fighting against that shit. I know we've got an obligation to Tôhô, but if you wanted to make a comeback, you should've gone up against the Starship Enterprise. And what about that scene with the flock of birds? When you turned your head to look at them and the scientist character said, "Godzilla's body has set up a magnetic resonance with the migrating birds. See, Godzilla too has a homing instinct." But that's not what happened this time, is it, brother? A pretty girl has turned your head.

GODZILLA: Well...I guess so.

YAYOI: Philanderer.

GODZILLA: Till I met you.

YAYOI: Well, you won't get away with that anymore.

GODZILLA: Honest to God, I promise...

MOTHRA: Now don't the two of you sound lovey-dovey. Give me a break! Did you ever imagine in your wildest dreams you'd be snuggling up to Godzilla? It ain't normal, girl.

YAYOI: I don't mind if it "ain't normal." So long as he's faithful.

MOTHRA: Don't change the subject, dammit! You think, because I'm Mothra, you can make a fool of me? *(MOTHRA spits out thread.)*

GODZILLA: Not the thread! Please no thread. When Mo' gets worked up, he starts spitting up thread.

MOTHRA: What can I say...?

YAYOI: It's okay.

GODZILLA: She doesn't know to be afraid of anybody or how to look down on them. That's why she could fall in love with me.

MOTHRA: I know how you feel, brother. But, listen, didn't our last movie teach you anything? Our family rolls their eyes up at us, we're the laughing stock of our monster buddies. Our day is over.

GODZILLA: Maybe so.

MOTHRA: So wise up.

GODZILLA: I have. We'll get married, settle down in our own place and have terrific kids.

MOTHRA: Marrying, settling down in your own new home—all that's just dandy. But don't you see, brother? It can't be. Till just a while ago, you were stomping buildings and snapping up bullet trains—that was bad, but this is unthinkable. Marrying this "girl"—you just can't! If you're a monster, behave like a monster and pick a monster bride.

GODZILLA: Mothy, falling in love with someone is not something you choose. It's only chance I happened to fall in love with a human being. If she were some sort of monster, I'm sure I'd love her just as much...

MOTHRA: Fine words, brother, but they don't fool me. Those are her words, not yours. You're not that sort of Godzilla. What if she were Namegon, would you still love her?

GODZILLA: Uh...sure.

MOTHRA: That sticky old slug? She'd cover you in slime. Ugh! Or what about Gamakujira, brother?

GODZILLA: If she were Yayoi, no problem.

MOTHRA: Get out of here! Gamakujira? All that croaking in the summer? Spouting water out her blow hole? How about Zora or Balloonga? Woo maybe? Or Zazahn...?

GODZILLA: So long as she's Yayoi.

MOTHRA: Come off it, brother! Say you've just got married—it's the first night, you're in bed and your new bride comes in and it's...Hedorah!* What would you do? I'm mean, she really *stinks*. Tell me the truth. You say you love this human girl Yayoi, right? You love everything about her? Her eyes, her mouth, her nose, ears, hands, fingers, arms, shoulders, the way she moves, her voice, each and every strand of hair?

GODZILLA: That's right.

MOTHRA: How long do you plan to keep up this façade? If you don't get a grip on yourself and move on with your life, before long nobody will have anything to do with you.

GODZILLA: But if I marry her, I'll be more responsible.

MOTHRA: ...I see. So, come hell or high water, you want to marry the girl.

GODZILLA: That's right, I can't live without her!

MOTHRA: I'm really sorry to hear that. "I can't live without her!" Give me a break. Is this the Godzilla who's not afraid of missiles or high power lines?

YAYOI: Please! We want to be together!

MOTHRA: Have you any notion what it means to be "together"?

YAYOI: Yes.

MOTHRA: What are you going to do to eat?

YAYOI: We'll go to the fields and pick fruit from the trees, we'll go to the sea and catch fish...

---

*Hedorah was an extraterrestrial monster that thrived on Japan's industrial pollution. 'She' was featured in *Godzilla vs. the Smog Monster* (1971).

MOTHRA: You just don't get it, do you? And you, brother, what are you going to do for work?

GODZILLA: Work?

MOTHRA: We're getting nowhere with this conversation. Just what the hell *have* you been doing these past three years?

GODZILLA: Aside from my acting career, Mothy, what sort of work did you have in mind?

MOTHRA: It's way too late to be talking about movies now—me, I've given up on 'em. Now I'm trying to make a living selling cocoons.

GODZILLA: How's business?

MOTHRA: Not so hot. What with all the fuss over the yen, the price of domestic products went way up and nobody's buying. Last month I couldn't even pay my bills. If it keeps up like this I won't be able to carry on. I'll just have to string myself up by the neck.

YAYOI: You have a neck, do you?

MOTHRA: You got a cute face, but you really know how to hurt a guy. For crissake, I'm a caterpillar. You think things are so bad I can't even kill myself?

GODZILLA: Times are tough, even for Big Mo'.

MOTHRA: It's the same everywhere. Gamera turned his shell into a hotel, made it into a island floating in the ocean. And Daimajin became a target at an amusement park. You can shoot soft rubber balls from a gun at him—every time a ball hits the target on his chest, he roars "*Gaaaooo.*"

GODZILLA: Tough all round, eh?

MOTHRA: You think this is easy? You don't know what you're in for. You'll have to support her, you know.

GODZILLA:	Well, we'll make do without money.
MOTHRA:	Make do? How? What'll you do if she gets sick? Got any health insurance?
YAYOI:	I won't get sick. Even if I do, I'll get better by myself.
MOTHRA:	Mighty brave of you.
YAYOI:	Thanks to him.
MOTHRA:	What'll you do if you have kids? All the school stuff—satchel, lunches—it costs lots of money, you know.
YAYOI:	I'll teach them myself.
MOTHRA:	They'll have no playmates, the poor things.
YAYOI:	If my children are really kind, they'll naturally attract lots of friends.
MOTHRA:	...This one's too good for you, brother.
GODZILLA:	I think so too. That's why I don't want to give her up...

Scene Ten
Monster Wife

PIGMON:	*(Entering.)* Honey? Where are you?
MOTHRA:	Over here!
PIGMON:	You're here too, brother?
GODZILLA:	Long time no see. You're looking well.
PIGMON:	No rest for the poor. Who's got time to be sick? Now, honey, you really ought to tell me when we've got guests. Least I can do is offer tea. Hey! Who's the girl?

MOTHRA: Oh, right, I'll introduce you. This is my wife, Pigmon.*

YAYOI: My name's Yayoi Ichinose. Pleased to meet you.

PIGMON: Nice kid. This is the first time a human's come up to me and given me a big smile.

YAYOI: So, Mothra, your wife's a monster too.

GODZILLA: Two birds of a feather, eh? Like Mothra, Pigmon always had a thing for humans. Mothra completely fell for that—they had something in common he could use to chat her up.

MOTHRA: "Fell for it"? Really, brother! *(Spews up thread.)*

GODZILLA: I'm begging you, Mothra, please! Stop!

PIGMON: Honey, we could've sold that! You're too old to be wasting thread like that. Save it for the factory!

MOTHRA: She's so annoying. The poorer us guys get, the stronger women become. As a movie, Mothra vs. Pigmon would've been no contest. But now we're a married couple, when we fight, I lose every time.

PIGMON: To what do we owe this unexpected pleasure? If it's money you need, sorry, but we can't even pay our own bills. Anything else, though, we'd be happy to oblige.

MOTHRA: He's getting married.

PIGMON: Well, well—congratulations. That's wonderful. So, who's the lucky girl? Ebirah? Gomorrah? Or Pagos, perhaps? Surely it couldn't be Balloonga. No, you wouldn't go for her—she's built like a boulder. How 'bout Jamira? You'd better forget about her, what with her reputation.

---

*Like Alien Valtan, Jamila, Gomorrah and Gamakujira, Pigmon was a character from the *Ultraman* TV series. Resembling somewhat a giant cockroach (but a cute one), 'she' was a friend of humans.

MOTHRA:	She's a he, stupid.
PIGMON:	What difference does it make? We're all monsters, after all—can't tell male from female. Hear what happened to Gomess and Hydra? They exchanged vows and it wasn't till their wedding night they noticed—both girls. What a scandal!
MOTHRA:	Godzilla wants to marry this person here.
PIGMON:	This person?
GODZILLA:	We'll be needing your help from time to time. I do hope you'll oblige.
YAYOI:	Yes, we hope you'll oblige.
PIGMON:	You're kidding.
GODZILLA:	I'm serious.
PIGMON:	You really must be joking.
MOTHRA:	I really wish they were.
PIGMON:	Godzilla and…this *girl*? Nah… *(Starts to leave.)*
MOTHRA:	Hey, hey, wait! Where are you going?
PIGMON:	Just remembered—I've got to go next door, to see Gabadon's wife.
MOTHRA:	Off she goes to yakety-yak to Garamon, Black King, Gappa and the rest of the girls.
PIGMON:	Well, this is big news after all.
MOTHRA:	Go ahead with your gabfest, but watch where you gather this time. When you guys were yammering away there on the Shônan Coast, they called in the UN forces.
YAYOI:	Pigmon, do you think we'll get along?
PIGMON:	Well… I've always had a thing for people—some

	of my best friends are humans—but the others are not so open-minded. Still, who's to say? So long as you're straight with us, I'm sure we'll get along.
YAYOI:	I'll do my best! Though I can't say I'm mad about bugs...
MOTHRA:	Tough luck, kid.
YAYOI:	Always had a soft spot for reptiles, though. Snakes and lizards—no problem.
PIGMON:	Lizards, eh? Close enough, I guess...
MOTHRA:	Fine. I'll do what I can to help you guys out.
GODZILLA:	Thanks, Mo'!
YAYOI:	Thank you very much!
MOTHRA:	So, what do you want from me?
GODZILLA:	We'd like you to be master of ceremonies at our wedding reception.
MOTHRA:	Emcee?

Scene Eleven
Wedding Party

MOTHRA is suddenly in tuxedo.

MOTHRA:	Welcome, everyone, and thanks for making the effort to be here today. And now, here come the bride and groom—give them a big hand, everybody!
	(Wedding March. Applause.) Ah, hang on a sec, brother. What are we going to do? You can't even link arms. You're fifty meters taller than the little lady.

YAYOI: Hold out your hand, Godzilla.

GODZILLA: Of course! *(GODZILLA puts YAYOI on the palm of his hand.)*

MOTHRA: Let us begin. We are gathered here together today to join these two houses, Godzilla and Ichinose, together. Now for the matchmaker...Uh, what about the go-between, brother? We need someone for the sake of form, at least.

PIGMON: Would Gappa do, I wonder?

MOTHRA: Not a good idea. He's with Nikkatsu—Tôhô Pictures won't be amused.

GODZILLA: How about Ultraman?

PIGMON: Nice choice. He's sort of a half-human and half-monster—perfect for a go-between.

MOTHRA: There's a bit of a problem, though.

PIGMON: How so?

MOTHRA: He only lasts three minutes. No sooner would he introduce the couple than, swoosh! He'd be gone.

GODZILLA: Oh right. We'll have to ask him to make just the speech, then.

YAYOI: "Ultraman's Three-Minute Speech!"

MOTHRA: That cute face of yours says the funniest things. Next, I'd like to call upon Gamera, standing in for the defunct Daiei Company, to congratulate the couple. Gamera, please.

GAMERA roars.

...A million-dollar voice. Thank you very much. And thanks to you all, folks, we have successfully wrapped up this ceremony joining the two *great* houses of Godzilla and Ichinose. And now, the

> bride and groom, full of gratitude, will present bouquets of flowers to their parents. Please give them another big hand!
>
> *FATHER, MOTHER and TSUBURAYA stand together. GODZILLA and YAYOI approach them.*

PIGMON: *(Reading a message from the bride.)* "Thank you, Dad, thank you, Mom, for all you've done to raise me. Today, my many relatives and friends will give me away to marry into Godzilla's family. Thanks, Mom, for teaching me that my destiny is to love all sentient beings. I give all my love to Godzilla. When was it, Daddy?—after dinner one evening, you put me on your knee and rubbed your scratchy beard up against my cheek and said 'the man who'll one day be your husband has to be strong and sturdy.' Now my husband is Godzilla—the strongest in the world!"

MOTHRA: Please let's give them another warm round of applause, everybody!

> *(Applause.)* And now to close, on behalf of the Godzilla and Ichinose families, Eiji Tsuburaya, president of Tsuburaya Productions and father of Godzilla, would like to express his gratitude to you all.
>
> *TSUBURAYA slowly proceeds, smiles and takes YAYOI's hand. Coming around to face GODZILLA, he tries to take GODZILLA's hand, but instead throws the bouquet of flowers into GODZILLA's face.*
>
> *Instantly the young couple's fantasy of their wedding party is broken and all the characters snap back into reality.*

MOTHRA: Dad!!

FATHER: Yayoi! Who said I'd give permission for your wedding!

YAYOI: Daddy!

TSUBURAYA: Forgive me for dragging out the family laundry here. Pleased to make your acquaintance. I'm this guy's dad, Eiji Tsuburaya.

FATHER: Your name's well known to us, sir. I'm Yayoi's father, Yôgan Ichinose, and this is my wife, Tsumugi.

MOTHER: Pleased to meet you.

TSUBURAYA: It seems my son's been an awful nuisance for you. I'm terribly sorry.

FATHER: No trouble at all—no victims, either.

MOTHER: We're not especially happy with our own child, either. She's a bit odd, you know.

TSUBURAYA: What are you saying, Mrs. Ichinose? Why, she's a fine young woman—she's positively radiant, inside and out. I envy you. This character may be family, but compared to her, he's a complete disgrace.

MOTHER: I really must disagree. Of all the great monsters of the world, Godzilla's the greatest.

TSUBURAYA: That's a thing of the past. He's no better than a gangster—he's got no job and spends his days loafing around. When he's bored he runs amok and bothers people. To have a son like this marry your precious daughter is really quite unacceptable. *(To GODZILLA.)* Apologize, boy! Crawl back to the mountains! Turn into a rock or something!

MOTHRA: Dad, could you just hear him out for a second?

TSUBURAYA: And who are you to lecture me, worm-boy? You've got no arms or legs.

MOTHRA spews out thread.

FATHER,
MOTHER,
TSUBURAYA: Ewww!!

PIGMON: How dare you! On your own dad!

MOTHRA: Sorry!

YAYOI: As you said, sir, Godzilla did act out a bit aggressively, but it's just that he was lonely. Everybody's afraid of him—not just people, but even his fellow monsters. Feared by all and without rival, Godzilla became lonelier and lonelier, till unable to bear the isolation any longer, he started misbehaving. Just look in his eyes. His body can withstand any cannon or missile used against it, but his heart's been shot, broken! It's been so traumatized it trembles, as vulnerable as an ant crawling on asphalt.

MOTHER: ...Yayoi.

YAYOI: Mummy, daddy, he needs me! Without me, he'll act up again. Next time, who knows how many buildings he'll smash or how many people he'll injure. Should that happen, though, he'll be so hurt nobody could ever heal his pain...and he would fall.

GODZILLA: Yayoi—

TSUBURAYA: Maybe Godzilla needs you, but why do you need Godzilla?

YAYOI: I think it's because I've got so much love in me that only Godzilla's a match for it all. Don't you think so? If my love weren't a hundred times, a thousand times what a mere man could stand, there's no way I could love a monster like Godzilla.

> *TSUBURAYA clutches at GODZILLA's chest and beats and kicks him badly.*

MOTHRA: Dad!

YAYOI: Mr. Tsuburaya!

FATHER: Mr. Tsuburaya, please! That's enough now!

TSUBURAYA: Do you see, Godzilla? I can punch you as hard as I can, and it doesn't hurt any more than a mosquito bite. I can kick you all day long, and you notice it less than a breeze blowing on your legs. Don't you see that you've already failed her? It's because you can't be hurt, you can't feel the kind of pain that would turn a human being into a quivering pool of his own blood and vomit. Until you understand how much you've hurt others—even hurt yourself—you can never make her happy.

GODZILLA: Dad...

TSUBURAYA: ...I'm leaving. I've got some business to attend to.

MOTHER: Do you have to rush off?

TSUBURAYA: Thanks to the Lucas and Spielberg boys, my stock's taken a real tumble these days. Maybe it's their special effects, but no way I'm going to take their brand of chicken-shit lying down! Just watch! One day soon, my kids will be trashing Tokyo again on the silver screen! I promise. And, uh...

FATHER: Yes?

TSUBURAYA: If, by any chance you did give your daughter to this boorish son of mine Godzilla, I'd be most grateful.

MOTHRA: Now didn't that turn out well, brother?

YAYOI: *(To TSUBURAYA.)* Thank you so much...Father.

TSUBURAYA: Well, I must be going. ...Young lady—

YAYOI: Yes?

TSUBURAYA: Yayoi—that's your name, right?

YAYOI: Yes.

TSUBURAYA: ...There, on your back...

YAYOI: Yes?

TSUBURAYA: So white, they're radiant ... They're wings, aren't they?

YAYOI: *(Smiling almost fiercely, she looks over her shoulder.)* Seems so.

FATHER: ...Godzilla.

GODZILLA: Yes?

FATHER: Could we, uh...?

MOTHER: We should leave them alone.

YAYOI: Yes.

MOTHRA: Hang in there big brother. I just want you to be happy!

Scene Twelve
Man to Man

    GODZILLA and FATHER. FATHER takes out his cigarettes.

FATHER: ...Smoke?

GODZILLA: No, thanks. Bad for the health.

FATHER: You don't mince words, do you? *(Tries to light up with his lighter but there's no flame.)* Shit! Out of fluid.

GODZILLA: Need a light? Allow me. *(About to spit fire.)*

FATHER: Aaaahh! You still don't get it, do you?

GODZILLA: Sorry.

FATHER: No, my mistake. I'm trying to quit. It *is* bad for the health, after all. What about the booze?

GODZILLA: Booze? Oh…actually, never tried.

FATHER: Well, I guess that makes sense. You can't go to the pub—I guess you're better off not getting a taste for the stuff. If you were to start, why, you'd drink up Japan's whole supply of saké in a single night and then there wouldn't be any left for me. Hah, hah!

GODZILLA: Sorry to disappoint you.

FATHER: Anyway, drinking's bad for the health. …But what about some mahjong or cards?

GODZILLA: What?

FATHER: Don't tell me you don't.

GODZILLA: I can't.

FATHER: You sure? Come on, I'll teach you. It's not so hard…

GODZILLA: I can't.

FATHER: Ah, I see what you mean. You'd pick up a whole casino with those fingers.

GODZILLA: Sorry.

FATHER: No problem. Gambling's bad for the health too.

GODZILLA: Sir, we…

FATHER: You know, I'm surrounded by women here. I wanted a son, but we ended up with three girls. I've longed for the day when I could hang out with my son-in-law. Just two guys drinking, playing mahjong, chewing the fat together, talking 'bout life—you know?

GODZILLA: Yes, let's talk about life, then. Why, in my own way, I've…

FATHER: In your own way? I mean, do you have a life, like the rest of us? All you ever do is follow your instincts, stomping on cities and flattening forests. What kind of life is that? You're telling me your future, or your work, or family matters get you down?—like they do the rest of us, like they do me? Are you telling me you can fall in love, madly in love with a woman—just like the rest of us?! Just becoming a kinder, gentler Godzilla won't make you a man. There's no way you can ever make my daughter happy!

GODZILLA: ...I'm very sorry.

FATHER: No, I should apologise. Got carried away there. I ought to know, it's bad for the health.

(He takes out his cigarettes again.) Smoke?

GODZILLA: No thanks, it's bad for the health.

FATHER: *(Tries to light his cigarette but can't strike a flame.)* Shit, out of fluid. Got a light?

GODZILLA: ...Sorry, don't smoke.

FATHER and GODZILLA smile at each other, two men with an understanding.

FATHER: That girl's our pride and joy. ...Make her happy, you hear?

GODZILLA: Yes, sir!

Scene Thirteen
Siege

The Technical Search Unit theme plays.

TWIN 2: First wave of Operation Godzilla, ready and waiting, Captain!

HAYATA:	Right, wait for the signal!
TWIN 2:	Roger!
TWIN 1:	Second wave of Operation Godzilla, ready and waiting, Captain!
HAYATA:	Wait for the signal! Command HQ here—tell us Godzilla's current position.
REPORTER:	Godzilla is currently located approximately one kilometre southwest of the port of Motomachi, at the Ichinose residence. No sign of movement, sir!
HAYATA:	Roger, carry on with your surveillance!
TWIN 2:	Captain, Command HQ Chief, approaching!
TWIN 1:	Attention!
GRANDMOTHER:	*(Entering.)* Any more sign of movement from Godzilla?
HAYATA:	Yes, sir! He's currently holed up approximately one kilometre southwest of the port of Motomachi, at the residence of one Yôgan Ichinose. Yôgan, his wife Tsumugi, and the eldest daughter Yayoi are still inside. Looks like they've been taken hostage.
GRANDMOTHER:	What in heaven's name does Godzilla have in mind?
TWIN 1:	We can't yet confirm this report, but it would seem that Godzilla is demanding the parents sacrifice their eldest daughter Yayoi to him.

YAYOI, MOTHER and FATHER burst in.

YAYOI:	Mr. Hayata! Would you please stop this foolishness!
MOTHER:	Mother! Why are you wrapped up in this?
HAYATA:	Don't worry, Dad! Operation Godzilla is ready and

	waiting to launch the attack! By air, crack Self-Defense Force team Blue Impulse; by land, the Police Mobile SWAT unit; and by sea, all the way from America, the Enterprise, flagship of the US Seventh Fleet, joining forces with the Technical Search Unit to destroy Godzilla!
FATHER:	That's enough now, Hatchan! I'm sorry it had to be this way for you, but…
HAYATA:	It's not enough! Who can tell when Godzilla will go off on another of his rampages? He's not just some drunken dad who beats his wife and kids, you know!
YAYOI:	Mr. Hayata, why don't you understand?
HAYATA:	What do you want me to understand, Yayoi? Just how can I stop loving you?—my love's like a fountain that keeps spilling from my cupped hands, I can't hold it back—not for anything, not even for your Godzilla.
YAYOI:	I'm much obliged to you, Mr. Hayata. I'm truly lucky to be loved so much. If only I could return your love, I know I'd be happy. But…
HAYATA:	But?
YAYOI:	I love Godzilla. If a single camellia were enough to return your love, still, I'd have to give much more than that—more than a tree full of countless camellia blossoms—to respond to Godzilla's love.
HAYATA:	Your love will surely save Godzilla, then. But now I've lost you, who in the world will save *me*, Yayoi, if you can't?
YAYOI:	Mr. Hayata, I'm not out to save anybody. I couldn't if I tried. How can repay my family and friends—even you—anyone who's ever sheltered me from all the evil that exists in this world? All I can do smile at Godzilla, who all the world fears, and at

every little thing he says and does, smile and love him for all I'm worth!

HAYATA: Permission to attack, Chief!

FATHER: Hayata!

MOTHER: Hayata!

GRANDMOTHER: Hatchan, are you sure this is right? Godzilla won't be the only one getting hurt here.

HAYATA: I'm aware of that!

YAYOI: Mr. Hayata, why? Why don't you understand?

GRANDMOTHER: Silence, Yayoi! This is a guy thing.

HAYATA: Godzilla, the whole world fears you. So, to vanquish you, I'll become the most fearsome man of all! Prepare to attack!

YAYOI: Stop! I don't want to see him get hurt anymore!

HAYATA: Fire!

> *The Technical Search Unit launches wave after wave of attack: violent explosions and flying fireworks fill the sky. GODZILLA advances one step after another, spitting fire, crushing whole neighbourhoods, burning forests.*

GRANDMOTHER: First assault, fall back!

HAYATA: First assault, fall back!

> *GODZILLA doesn't flinch from any of the attacks, though his eyes are filled with an unfathomable sadness and he appears about to collapse any time.*

REPORTER: It's all over, Captain! We've thrown everything at him, but he's destroyed it all!

GRANDMOTHER: Give up, Hatchan. Any further attacks would only provoke Godzilla to inflict more harm.

HAYATA:	...Permission to transform, Chief!
TWINS & REPORTER:	Trooper Hayata!
GRANDMOTHER:	Is that really necessary?!
HAYATA:	If I give up now, my love can never be any more than what it already is. If I give up now, Yayoi can never be any more than who she is now!

HAYATA transforms into ULTRAMAN. GODZILLA vs. ULTRAMAN: a violent battle ensues, each one having the upper hand in turn. Then, ULTRAMAN, exhausted, falls. But it is GODZILLA who has been really hurt.

YAYOI:	Mr. Hayata, are you all right?
HAYATA:	Don't touch me! Please, no more sweet-talk from you. Your gentleness has hurt me and torn my heart to pieces more than any of the wounds he's inflicted.
FATHER:	Hatchan, that's enough, surely.
GRANDMOTHER:	Haven't you done enough, Hatchan? You've discharged your love for Yayoi till the bitter end. Now, Yayoi, go take Godzilla back to the mountain. None of us will speak against you. I won't let them.
FATHER:	Good luck, Yayoi.
MOTHER:	Take care of yourself, Yayoi.
TWINS:	Farewell, Yayoi.
YAYOI:	Thanks, Grandma. Thanks Daddy, Mummy, Emi, Yumi. Thank you all. Are you ready, Godzilla? Let's go. Are you wounded? Once we're back on the mountain, I'll tend your wounds.
GODZILLA:	...Don't come near. *(YAYOI is shocked.)* Back off!

YAYOI:	What's wrong, Godzilla? They have accepted us.
GODZILLA:	Do you want to be stepped on?

> *In contrast to his body language, GODZILLA's eyes are gentle.*

YAYOI:	…You, you can't say that!
GODZILLA:	Yayoi, we… Let's call it off. I don't want to make you unhappy, so let's call it off. I don't think I've got the faith to go on loving you. Not the way I am…not anymore.
YAYOI:	Godzilla…
GODZILLA:	If your skin weren't so pure and soft, but were covered in dark cracks; if you were ten times taller and and had a tail and could spit fire—in short, if you were a Godzilla like me—then, I'm sure things would work out.
HAYATA:	No! What were we fighting for? You can't abandon her, I won't let you! *(Trains his gun on GODZILLA.)*
GODZILLA:	*(To YAYOI.)* See?
GRANDMOTHER:	Hatchan!
MOTHER:	Hayata!
YAYOI:	*(Still not understanding.)* See?

> *GODZILLA slowly approaches the gun HAYATA is pointing at him.*

HAYATA:	You're not fooling me!

> *A loud bang. The bullet hits GODZILLA squarely in the chest.*

GODZILLA:	Felled at last by a puny little bullet, I can start all over and love you anew. I can't love you unless I stop being Godzilla and become somehow human

instead, somebody who can die from a single shot to my chest. So let this blood of mine that gushes from my breast—this blood that flows like my love for you, unceasingly—pour out till there's none left in my body. Let this blood I shed be my first promise to you that I'll no longer be Godzilla.

YAYOI: You're wrong, Godzilla. It wasn't a human Godzilla I loved, but the fifty-meter-tall, three-hundred-ton, one-hundred-meter-long, fire-breathing Godzilla, strongest in the world!

GODZILLA slowly rises. The blood dripping from his breast is brilliant and yet heart-rending, like the petals of a camellia.

YAYOI: Where...where are you going?

GODZILLA: Back to the mountain.

YAYOI: Take me with you, please.

GODZILLA: Please don't follow me.

YAYOI: Why not?

GODZILLA: My heart's human, but even so, I'm still Godzilla...

The wounded GODZILLA slowly begins to move away. Only YAYOI remains. The stage goes dark. Far off, a resounding explosion.

YAYOI: ...Where will you go if you leave me, Godzilla? Must I stand here and watch you leave, knowing how defenceless you've become? Do you have any idea how I feel, Godzilla? How can you walk away, impassive as always, shedding no tears at all, and make me so unhappy? The mountains weep for me and I cannot wipe those tears away. The woods and grassy fields, this very earth, they always cared for the two of us; they all cry out now and weep bitterly because you're leaving me. And see, even the mountain gushes a stream of red-hot tears, all because of your heartless farewell!

> *Exhausted from speaking, YAYOI is silent. Having said all she wants to say, she realizes how much pain she has inflicted on herself and others simply by smiling back like an angel.*

Scene Fourteen
The Pier II

> *An unsettled atmosphere of cacophonous sounds: boat whistles, waves, traffic, sirens… The port of Oshima Motomachi. In the evening darkness, a woman looks up at Mt. Mihara, seen only faintly in silhouette.*
>
> *The woman, her heart wounded for the first time in her life, stands buffeted by the wind off the sea. Her cheeks wet with tears, she appears completely happy with the dry caress of the breeze.*
>
> *A resounding siren drowns out all the other sounds, sending sorrowful shudders through the heart and presaging a sublime climax to the play.*

HAYATA: The boat will soon sail. Everybody, please board quickly and in an orderly fashion.

MOTHRA: Officer, what'll happen…to the island?

HAYATA: No one knows.

FATHER: *(Shouting.)* Hurry up!

MOTHER: Don't dawdle, children! Hurry!

REPORTER: Reporting from Oshima Motomachi. It's been twelve years since the great eruption of Mt. Mihara and for three days now a swath of lava, dozens of meters wide, has poured from the outer crater with no sign of letting up. It's toppled forests and is now less than a kilometre southwest of the port of Motomachi. The last of the island's refugees are boarding the rescue ship Katori. At the end of this broadcast we members of the press too will evacuate.

GRANDMOTHER: Yayoi, what are you doing?

MOTHER: And without an umbrella while it's raining ashes like this! Here. *(Hands YAYOI a red umbrella.)*

TWINS: Daddy, hurry up!

YAYOI: What about Godzilla, mummy?

FATHER: Godzilla?

The violent sound of the eruption masks a distant roar.

FATHER, MOTHER & GRANDMOTHER: Huh?

TWINS: Hurry, let's go!

GRANDMOTHER: Hurry up, girl! Come on, enough foolishness now.

FATHER: Hurry up.

FATHER, MOTHER, GRANDMOTHER and TWINS board the boat.

HAYATA: The boat's about to leave, Yayoi. Don't miss it! I'll wait up for you.

YAYOI slowly opens her red umbrella. The scorched mountain, which will always watch over her, groans with tremors that only now begin to subside. Suddenly, there is a sign of life behind YAYOI. A MAN glances at her as he slips past her and tries to board the ship.

YAYOI: …Godzilla!

MAN: …Huh?

> Through the roar of the volcano, the MAN cannot clearly hear her from behind; he turns around. Failing to recognize her, he begins to leave.

YAYOI: …Godzilla.

> The MAN turns around once more, sure for the first time that he is being addressed. He slowly holds his hand out to the woman.

MAN: Hurry. …We'll escape together.

> YAYOI takes his hand and once again bids farewell to the mountain. She turns to face the MAN; he looks at her and they smile at each other. The pain in YAYOI's heart is suddenly healed and the faces of these two young people are radiant with burgeoning love. The MAN clasps her hand and leads her away. But there is no promise of happiness in their destination.

> Suddenly, there is a huge eruption that is nearly enough to send Oshima Island into the sea. The lava shoots hundreds of meters into the sky; there are embers flying everywhere, like some scene of the end of the world. The eruption's roar is just like GODZILLA's voice…

The End